Physical Health Benefits of Church

- Going to church every week makes you **20 to 30 percent less likely to die** in the next fifteen years.
- People who go to church every week when they are age twenty live on average **seven years longer** than people who never attend religious services.
- Weekly church is **as good for you as eating more fruits and vegetables**.
- Weekly church is *almost* **as good for you as quitting smoking or starting to exercise**![1]

[1] For more information on this, see the data discussed in my book, *How Church Could (Literally) Save Your Life* (Crossway, 2025).

What's more, when Jesus rose again, he beat death for us. So, anyone who now trusts in Jesus can live with him forever!

Are You Ready to Die?

Perhaps you don't believe in God. You think you'll simply stop existing when you die. But if that's true, your life is meaningless. You and everyone you love are just atoms and molecules. Deep down, we all know that's not true. The Bible says you're not just atoms. You were handmade by God to live in love with him forever.

Perhaps you do believe in God, and you think God will welcome you to heaven when you die. But according to the Bible, none of us deserves to live with God. All of us have sinned and we deserve God's judgment.

Being better than a lot of other people isn't good enough. Identifying as a Christian isn't good

Trust Me, I'm the Doctor

At some point in our lives, we'll all need a doctor. We might go to the doctor because we know we're sick. Or we might go for an annual checkup and find out we're sick. In the Bible, Jesus says he is the Doctor sent by God, and we all need him desperately.

One time, Jesus called a man named Matthew to follow him. Everybody knew Matthew was a sinner, not a good person. But Matthew agreed to follow Jesus, and he invited Jesus over to his house. So, Jesus had dinner with Matthew and his sinful friends.

The religious leaders of that day were shocked. They asked Jesus's followers, "Why is your teacher eating with sinners?" If Jesus had been sent by God, surely he'd want to spend his time with good (or "righteous") people, not with sinners!

But Jesus replied, "It is not the healthy who need a doctor, but the sick. I have not come to call the righteous, but sinners" (Mark 2:17 NIV).

Are You Healthy or Sick?

I wonder where you see yourself in this story.

Perhaps you see yourself as a good person—not perfect, but good enough to be on the right side of God, if God exists. That's how a lot of people think. But Jesus diagnoses all of us with spiritual sickness. This is the bad news of Christianity. We're all sinners who deserve God's judgment. The Bible says that "all have sinned and fall short of the glory of God" (Romans 3:23 NIV).

But the good news of Christianity is that Jesus didn't come for good people. He is the Doctor sent by God for sinners just like us! When Jesus died on a cross two thousand years ago, he took the judgment we deserve, so that *anyone* who trusts in him can be forgiven and made right with God.

enough. Going to church each week isn't good enough. Only Jesus—God's own Son—is good enough for God, and we will only be forgiven by God if we admit that we're not good enough for him and turn to Jesus. Like a doctor giving us a heart transplant, Jesus can save us.

If you are ready to admit you're spiritually sick, then Jesus came into this world *for you*. He gave up his life on the cross *for you*. He rose again to welcome you to live with him forever. And if you turn to him, he will send you his Holy Spirit so that your new life can start now!

Are You Ready to Live?

If you have lots of questions and don't feel ready to accept Jesus's offer, why not find a local church where you can ask your questions and explore more?

Mental Health Benefits of Church

- People who go to church each week are **33 percent less likely to get depressed**, and more likely to recover from depression.
- In America, adults who go to church regularly are **11 percent more likely to be "very happy."**
- Kids who go to church weekly are **less likely to get depressed or take illegal drugs** and more likely to become happy, healthy, caring adults.
- Weekly churchgoers are **50 percent less likely to die from suicide, drugs, or alcohol** than people who never attend church.

If you want to trust in Jesus now, here's a prayer you could pray:

Dear God,

I know I'm spiritually sick. I'm not a good person, and I don't deserve your love. But I know that Jesus came to die for people just like me and that he promised full forgiveness, eternal life, and love to anyone who trusts in him.

Thank you that you sent your Son to die for me. Thank you that you raised him from the dead and that he's beaten death for me so that I can live with him forever.

I'm sorry for living my life against you. I want to put my life in Jesus's hands and live with Jesus as my Lord. I know that will mean a lot of changes in my life. But if Jesus loves so much that he died for me, I'm going to trust that he knows what is best for me.

Please help me find a church where I can meet other people who have put their trust in Jesus, so we can live together with you as our Lord and help one another.

Amen.

If you have prayed that prayer, the next step is to join a local church. The people whom you will meet at church are not perfect people. They're sick people who have put their lives in the great Doctor's hands. And according to the Bible they're your new family.

To find a church near you where people will be glad to welcome you and help you on your journey, go to www.thekellercenter.org/findachurch.

If you've never been to church and don't know what to expect, that website will answer questions about what to wear, whether people expect you to know prayers or songs, how long the service will last, whether it is OK to bring noisy kids,